The Faith of Helen Keller

→ THE FAITH
OF HELEN KELLER

The Life of a Great
Woman, With Selections
From Her Writings

Edited by Jack Belck

081

HALLMARK EDITIONS

Contents

The Life of Helen Keller

7

Selected Writings:

On Herself

17

On Happiness

23

On Faith

27

In the Garden of the Lord

31

On People and Life

39

On Spring

47

On Easter

51

On Christmas

55

The Faith of Helen Keller

The Life of Helen Keller

Helen Keller, Mark Twain once said, is one of the two greatest women who ever lived.

The other, Twain believed, was Joan of Arc, the young French girl who led an army to victory because she believed God had called her to command.

A faith as strong and enduring as Joan's marks the life and career of Helen Keller.

Helen was born in Tuscumbia, Alabama in 1880. "The beginning of my life was simple and much like every other little life," she said. "I came, I saw, I conquered, as the first baby in the family always does."

Nineteen months later conquest changed to defeat with a suddenness that stunned: Helen, victim of an undiagnosed disease, was struck totally blind and deaf.

Up to this time, the little girl had shown a quick mind and the joy in life that only the very young can know. Now she was plunged into an empty, cold blackness, which even the sound of a human voice could not penetrate.

"I felt as if invisible hands were holding me, and I made frantic efforts to free myself," she wrote many years later. "I struggled—not that struggling helped matters, but the spirit of resistance was strong within me. I generally broke down in tears and physical exhaustion."

Unable to hear herself, she no longer chanted newly-learned words. They disappeared one by one until only the word "water" was left. That soon reverted to "wah-wah," and finally ceased too. Except for inarticulate cries, the small voice was still.

Her father and mother began to despair, for they remembered when their daughter had been an alert, bright child.

Trapped inside herself, Helen Keller felt that something was wrong even if she had no memories of the lights and sounds she had known as a baby. "I do not remember when I first realized that I was different from other people," she writes, "but I knew it before my teacher came to me. My mother and my friends did not use signs when they wanted anything done, but talked with their mouths. Sometimes I stood between two persons who were

8

conversing and touched their lips. I could not understand, and was vexed."

After five years of darkness and silence, something happened that would change Helen's life. Her mother, reading some writings of Charles Dickens, discovered there were places that might help the deaf-blind. One such place was in Boston, but that was far from Tuscumbia, Alabama. However, Mrs. Keller contacted the school and a meeting was arranged. Meeting led to meeting, consultation to consultation, and then one day Helen Keller met Dr. Alexander Graham Bell, inventor, teacher, and helper of those who could not see or hear.

Dr. Bell, impressed with the young child's problem, arranged for Miss Anne Sullivan to meet the Kellers. Anne would share most of the next fifty years with Helen as teacher, companion, friend—and pupil. Anne Sullivan, "the miracle worker," came to the Keller home when she was just twenty-one.

"The most important day I remember in all my life is the one on which my teacher came to me," Helen wrote later. Anne Sullivan knew about blindness. She had been a student at the Perkins Institute in Boston because of her own poor vision, and then she had gone on to learn how to help others who could see even less than she.

With determination, insight and compassion,

Anne literally took young, rebellious Helen Keller by the hand and led her into life.

Tapping the letters of the manual alphabet into the little girl's hand, Anne would spell out the word for the object her pupil had just touched. At first, word associations were difficult to make. But one day "Teacher"—as Helen ever after called her loving friend—poured cold water over Helen's hand and then spelled out "W-A-T-E-R." The connection between things and their names abruptly became clear. The sequence of tappings was the cold wetness on Helen's hand: W-A-T-E-R.

"That living word awakened my soul, gave it light, hope, joy, set it free! There were barriers still, it is true, but barriers that could in time be swept away."

Water. The last word lost was the first word learned. From then on, Helen Keller learned rapidly, eagerly. In June, 1887, only three months after Teacher's arrival, she wrote her first letter in time-consuming, tedious braille:

> Helen write anna george will give
> helen apples simpson will shoot
> bird jack will give helen stick of
> candy. . . .

Eight months later, under the steady direction

10

of Teacher, Helen's grasp of the English language
became more firm:

> My Dear Mr. Anagnos—
> I am glad to write you a letter in
> braille. This morning Lucien
> Thompson sent me a beautiful
> bouquet of violets and crocuses and
> jonquils . . . .

With the world of books partly opened to her,
Helen made up her mind to learn to speak. She
knew the difficulty it would involve for someone
who could neither see nor hear. But she felt she
must learn to talk, for the restriction of tapping
out her words in others' palms frustrated her:

> I can remember the time before I
> learned to speak . . . . I used to
> struggle to express my thoughts by
> means of the manual alphabet—
> how my thoughts used to beat a-
> gainst my fingertips like little birds
> striving to gain their freedom!

Although Helen's vitality and determination
could never fully overcome her handicaps, she did
learn to speak—and in several languages. Her

words sounded strange to the listener's ear, and she was unable to engage in spur-of-the-moment, casual conversation. But she learned to communicate orally with others.

With the help first of braille, then a braille machine, and later a typewriter, this remarkable woman expressed her feelings, opinions, and observations to a world that was fascinated by her achievement.

Her writings were only part of her unique career. She and her companion toured the United States, lecturing, visiting, talking, and praying for the handicapped.

She became famous, but fortune did not follow fame. Fees from appearances and lectures on behalf of the handicapped were used to help others — and to pay her bills.

She became a friend of Mark Twain and of Dr. Alexander Graham Bell. She talked with kings and queens of Europe, and with Presidents Wilson, Coolidge, Franklin Roosevelt and Eisenhower. But she never lost touch with those whose increased well-being she considered her special purpose in life: the blind poor.

Today, with many books, articles, essays, and lectures to her credit, she is regarded more as a great human being and humanitarian than as some sort of special, fascinating peculiarity.

To anyone who even briefly closes his eyes and blocks his ears to imitate Helen Keller's strange world, the imprisonment of being deaf and blind seems permanent and inescapable. But Helen Keller escaped her prison. Not only did she struggle out of her awful darkness and silence; she also learned to hope, to trust, to love—and to be happy.

The writings of Helen Keller serve to illuminate her own being and to help others see themselves. The selections in this book were chosen for their range of expression and interest. They show Miss Keller in moments of serenity, happiness, and appreciation of all living things.

Selected Writings

On Herself

They took away what should have been my eyes,
 (But I remembered Milton's Paradise).
They took away what should have been my ears,
 (Beethoven came and wiped away my tears).
They took away what should have been my tongue,
 (But I had talked with God when I was young).
 He would not let them take away my soul—
 Possessing that, I still possess the whole.

17

My life is a chronicle of friendship. My friends—all those about me—create my world anew each day. Without their loving care all the courage I could summon would not suffice to keep my heart strong for life. But, like Robert Louis Stevenson, I know it is better to do things than to imagine them.

My hand is to me what your hearing and sight together are to you . . . . All my comings and goings turn on the hand as a pivot. It is the hand that binds me to the world of men and women. The hand is my feeler with which I reach through isolation and darkness and seize every pleasure, every activity that my fingers encounter.

I, too, may construct my better world, for I am a child of God, an inheritor of a fragment of the Mind that created all worlds.

It is not possible for civilization to flow backward while there is youth in the world.

I try to increase the power God has given me to see the best in everything and everyone, and make that best a part of my life. The world is sown with good; but unless I turn my glad thoughts into practical living and till my own field, I cannot reap a kernel of the good.

A good cry yesterday morning washed away some of the shadows from my soul, so that I am able to see more of life's brightness and to chat with a few people.

I can't imagine a man wanting to marry me. I should think it would seem like marrying a statue.

We were always amused at the newspaper accounts of our appearance in a place. I was hailed as a princess and a prima donna and a priestess of the light. I learned for the first time that I was born blind, deaf and dumb; that I had educated myself; that I could distinguish colors, hear telephone messages, predict when it was going to rain; that I was never sad, never discouraged, never pessimistic; that I applied myself with celestial energy to being happy, that I could do anything that anybody with all his faculties could do. They said this was miraculous—and no wonder. We supplied the particulars when we were asked for them; but we never knew what became of the facts.

The reason why God permitted me to lose both sight and hearing seems clear now—that through me He might cleave a rock unbroken before and let quickening streams flow through other lives desolate as my own once was. I am content.

It would be wonderful to find myself free from even a small part of my physical limitations . . . to walk around town alone . . . to come and go without a word to anyone . . . to read the newspapers without waiting, and pick out a pretty handkerchief or a becoming hat in the shops.

I trust, and nothing that happens disturbs my trust. I recognize the beneficence of the power which we all worship as supreme—Order, Fate, the Great Spirit, Nature, God. I recognize this power in the sun that makes all things grow and keeps life afoot. I make a friend of this indefinable force, and straightway feel glad, brave, and ready for any lot heaven may decree for me. This is my religion of optimism.

The conflict between the artistic impulse and the calculating scientific tendency in modern times repels me—a future civilization is likely to be hard, practical, monotonous. I feel fortunate indeed that it has been possible for me to be a barbarian, to enjoy sculpture, poetry, happy make-believe in bleak corners of my limitations. It seems to me more urgent than ever to foster in the present young generation a spiritual philosophy and imagination that shall keep the morning dew in their souls when an age arrives that knows not the muses.

It is not true that I am never sad or rebellious; but long ago I determined not to complain. The mortally wounded must strive to live out their days cheerfully for the sake of others. That is what religion is for—to keep the heart brave to fight it out to the end with a smiling face. This may not be a very lofty ambition, but it is a far cry from surrendering to fate.

I believe that no good shall be lost, and that all man has willed or hoped or dreamed of good shall exist forever.

For three things I thank God every day of my life —that He has vouchsafed my knowledge of His works, deep thanks that He has set in my darkness the lamp of faith, deep, deepest thanks that I have another life to look forward to—a life joyous with light and flowers and heavenly song.

It is curious how thoughts behave. They elude me in a crowd. Like spirits, they must be spoken to in solitude before they will explain themselves.

On Happiness

*Joy is the holy fire that keeps our purpose warm
and our intelligence aglow. Work without joy
shall be as nothing. Resolve to keep happy,
and your joy and you shall form an invincible
host against difficulties.*

When one door of happiness closes, another opens; but often we look so long at the closed door that we do not see the one which has been opened for us.

Every human being has undeniable rights which, respected, render happiness possible—the right to live his own life as far as may be, to choose his own creed, to develop his capabilities; but no one has a right to consume happiness without producing it or to lay his burden upon other shoulders merely to fulfill a personal desire.

If those who seek happiness would only stop one little minute and think, they would see that the delights they really experience are as countless as the grasses at their feet or the dewdrops sparkling upon the morning flowers.

Resolve to keep happy. Fears and regrets have no place in the vocabulary of youth, whose spirit sets its white and shining wings toward the purple shores of the Promised Land.

Many persons have a wrong idea of what constitutes happiness. It isn't attained through self-gratification but through fidelity to a worthy purpose. Happiness should be a means of accomplishment, like health, not an end in itself.

Be happy, talk happiness. Happiness calls out responsive gladness in others. There is enough sadness in the world without yours. Rebel against the hardness and justice of things as much as you like.

Be happy, talk happiness. It is always well to keep your fighting edge keen to smite wrongs whenever you meet them. But never doubt the excellence and permanence of what is yet to be.

Certainly I believe that God gave us life for happiness, not misery. Humanity, I am sure, will never be made lazy or indifferent by an excess of happiness. The order of nature will always necessitate pain, failure, separation, death; and these will probably become more menacing as the complexities and dangerous experiments of a vast world civilization increase.

Your success and happiness lie in you. External conditions are the accidents of life, its outer trappings. The great, enduring qualities are love and service.

On Faith

*Faith refuses to be confined to one path. It
will break through any wilderness regardless of
every restraint except the Law of Life,
untroubled by conditions but creating the
next state by its discoveries.*

A simple, childlike faith in a Divine Friend solves all the problems that come to us by land or sea.

Faith is mental perception of what is good, together with a steady endeavor to live despite all obstacles.

Faith teaches us to use our talents to the fullest extent, however slight they may be. Faith is a responsibility for us as well as a privilege.

Religion is the fruit of faith, and to ask for religion without faith is like asking for the flower without the seed. Many religions have spread inspiring hope upon earth, but one Faith has been their tree, just as goodwill is the one root of all truly beneficent activities.

Faith does not oblige us to be unusually endowed, but receptive. To say others may have it but we cannot is wanton self-limitation. To be alert for whatever surprises may glow within us is to have at our command a zest for living which outweighs all material possessions.

Faith sanctifies any place, renders its climate bracing to weakness, its air luminous to doubt-dimmed eyes. Continents sink; empires disintegrate; but faith and the universe of heroic minds abide forever.

Faith has such might because next to love it is the force most inherent in one's own awareness. It directs to the light when darkness prevails; it supplies incentive to action and converts ideas into realities. It fires the imagination, and this is essential, for one must envision the higher life and behave as if it were a fact before it can unfold. But though faith belongs to the future, its energy irradiates the present, just as the green leaf pigment—the delicate link between the sun and life—permeates the vegetable world.

Faith, like philosophy, endows me with a unity I miss in the chaos of material experience devoid of sight and hearing. But like everyone else I have eyes in my soul. Through faith I create the world I gaze upon; I make my own day and night, tint the clouds with iridescent fires, and behold! a midnight is strewn with other stars.

It is faith which lights us into sustaining realities beyond those perceived by the physical senses.

Faith transmutes circumstance, time, condition and mood into vitality. This is why Christ's teaching was momentously effective nineteen centuries ago and still is so today among those who truly respond to it.

In the Garden of the Lord

*Even more amazing than the wonders of
nature are the powers of the spirit.*

Hold out your hands to feel the luxury of the sunbeams. Press the soft blossoms against your cheek, and finger their graces of form, their delicate mutability of shape, their pliancy and freshness. Expose your face to the aerial floods that sweep the heavens, "inhale great draughts of space," wonder, wonder at the wind's unwearied activity. Pile note on note the infinite music that flows increasingly to your soul from the tactual sonorities of a thousand branches and rumbling waters .... I am sure that if a fairy bade me choose between the sense of sight and that of touch, I would not part with the warm, endearing contact of human hands or the wealth of form, the mobility and fullness that press into my palms.

I believe that only in broken gleams has the Sun of Truth yet shone upon men. I believe that love will finally establish the Kingdom of God on earth, and that cornerstones of that Kingdom will be Liberty, Truth, Brotherhood, and Service.

I believe that we can live on earth according to the fulfillment of God's will, and that when the will of God is done on earth as it is in heaven, every man will love his fellow men and act toward them as he desires they should act toward him. I believe that the welfare of each is bound up in the welfare of all.

Any life assumes true nobility and significance only when one believes that one is born into the world for ends higher than any which can be reached within the narrow limits of earthly existence.

I believe that we can live on earth according to the teachings of Jesus, and that the greatest happiness will come to the world when man obeys His commandment, that "ye love one another."

I believe that life is given us so we may grow in love, and I believe that God is in me as the sun is in the color and fragrance of a flower—the Light in my darkness, the Voice in my silence.

Sick or well, blind or seeing, bound or free, we are here for a purpose and however we are situated, we please God better with useful deeds than with many prayers or pious resignation.

Often when the heart is torn with sorrow, spiritually we wander like a traveller lost in a deep wood. We grow frightened, lose all sense of direction, batter ourselves against trees and rocks in our attempt to find a path. All the while there is a path—the path of Faith—that leads straight out of the dense tangle of our difficulties into the open road we are seeking.

Only religion which evenly blends the personal gospel and the social gospel can endure or keep the church alive.

The word of God came unto me,
Sitting alone among the multitudes;
And my blind eyes were touched with light.
And there was laid upon my lips a flame of fire.

I laugh and shout for life is good,
Though my feet are set in silent ways.
In merry mood I leave the crowd
To walk in my garden. Ever as I walk
I gather fruits and flowers in my hands.
And with joyful heart I bless the sun
That kindles all the place with radiant life.

I run with playful winds that blow the scent
Of rose and jessamine in eddying whirls.
At last I come where tall lilies grow,
Lifting their faces like white saints to God.
While the lilies pray, I kneel upon the ground;
I have strayed into the temple of the Lord.

Let us go back to keep alive the gleam,
To cherish the immortal, godlike dream,
Not as poor cravens flying from the fight,
But as sad children seeking the clean light.

We have a Friend who "slumbers not, nor sleeps," and who watches over us and guides us—if we but let Him. With this thought strongly entrenched in our inmost being, we can do almost anything we wish and need not limit the things we think. We may help ourselves to all the beauty of the universe that we can hold.

I realize that mortals are only tiny drops lost in an ocean of time. The most any race or individual can do is enter a little more deeply into the purpose of the Divine Mind. That race, that individual, fulfills the highest destiny that is the best medium to transmit the current of goodwill through the ages.

Experiencing a great sorrow is like entering a cave. We are overwhelmed by the darkness, the loneliness, the homesickness. Sad thoughts, like bats, flutter about us in the gloom. We feel that there is no escape from the prison house of pain. But God in His Loving-Kindness has set on the invisible wall the Lamp of Faith—whose beams shall guide us back to the sunlit world where work and friends and service await us.

I believe that every question between man and man is a religious question, and that every social wrong is a moral wrong.

There is another sustaining belief in me—that a watchful Providence guides equally the planet's course and the flight of the sparrow, marks human affairs and strengthens endeavor. This faith that God is "personally" interested in us gives a fairer aspect to the weary old world where we live as strangers and enemies. It imparts to those who can believe a consciousness of power. It lets them be sure that mankind *can* prevail against the snares, machinations and greed of the wicked. Knowing that the hosts of the Lord encamp about them, they fear not armies or navies or lines of defense. Confidently, they tell themselves that one day all men *will* be lovers and human calamities will vanish in the sunshine of peace and goodwill upon earth.

We wake to see with new eyes and hear with new ears the beauty and harmony of God's real world.

Surely we would not weep if some beloved friend had the good fortune to move from a humble and uncomfortable house to a mansion into which the sunlight streamed, and whose grounds are a never-ending maze of beauty and wonder and delight. We would say that that was a fortunate friend, and, a bit wistfully, we would look forward to the time when we too might leave the burden of our daily tasks and join him in his house of beauty and light.

Other feet have traveled that road before me, and I know the desert leads to God as surely as the green, refreshing fields and fruitful orchards. God, I have heard it said, is the sum of the best aspirations and wisest thoughts and most beautiful actions of mankind. God is truly this sum, since He gives these things to man, but He is far beyond all of them and will forever be beyond the highest man achieves, just as love and moral progress and beauty in art will forever lie beyond what man is able to attain.

Without some kind of God, man could not have survived toiling under crushing loads pierced by glacial cold, scorched by desert suns, seeing his loved ones slain or ravished or dying of hunger! He remains primitive, as related to the unmeasured new forces he is discovering. Still handicapped by ignoble instincts and superstition, he needs increasingly an open-eyed faith in a beneficent power with whom he may cooperate to overcome and create. This force alone can prevent him from disappearing in a cataclysm, "annihilated by his own foolishness."

On People and Life

*It is beyond a doubt that everyone should have
time for some special delight, if only five
minutes each day to seek out a lovely flower
or cloud or a star, or learn a verse or brighten
another's dull task. What is the use of such terrible
diligence as many tire themselves out with, if
they always postpone their exchange of smiles
with Beauty and Joy to cling to irksome duties
and relations?*

Anyone who, out of the goodness of his heart, speaks a helpful word, gives a cheering smile, or smooths over a rough place in another's path knows that the delight he feels is so intimate a part of himself that he lives by it.

There are red-letter days in our lives when we meet people who thrill us like a fine poem, people whose handshake is brimful of unspoken sympathy, and whose sweet, rich natures impart to our eager, impatient spirits a wonderful restfulness which, in its essence, is divine . . . . Perhaps we never saw them before, and they may never cross our life's path again; but the influence of their calm, mellow natures is a libation poured upon our discontent, and we feel its healing touch, as the ocean feels the mountain stream freshening its brine.

Each lives according to convictions for which he would willingly lay down his life, and at the same time he hinders his advancement by not cultivating fundamental ethics.

Individuals become strong only in proportion to the spiritual growth of their own development.

In daily intercourse and literature, words of fault-finding outnumber words of good-finding.

It is wonderful how much time good people spend fighting the devil. If they would only expend the same amount of energy loving their fellow men, the devil would die of ennui.

I often think that beautiful ideas embarrass most people as much as the company of great men. There is no king who has not had a slave among his ancestors, and no slave who has not had a king among his.

Youth may be headstrong, but it will advance its allotted length. Through the ages in the battle with the powers of evil—with poverty, misery, ignorance, war, ugliness, and slavery—youth has steadily turned on the enemy. That is why I never turn away from the new generation impatiently because of its knowingness. Through it alone shall salvation come.

More is gained by the mistakes of those who honestly try to think for themselves than by the correct opinions of those who hold them simply because they have not heard the other side.

When we do the best we can, we never know what miracle is wrought in our life, or in the life of another.

I am blind and have never seen a rainbow, but I have been told of its beauty. I know that its beauty is always broken and incomplete. Never does it stretch across the heavens in full perfection. So it is with all things as we know them here below. Life itself is as imperfect and broken for every one of us as the span of the rainbow. Not until we have taken the step from life into Eternity shall we understand the meaning of Browning's words: "On the earth the broken arcs; in the heaven, a perfect round."

The most important question is not the sort of environment we have but the kind of thoughts we think every day, the kind of ideals we are following; in a word, the kind of men and women we really are . . . .

Join the great company of those who make the barren places of life fruitful with kindness.

The joy of surmounting obstacles which once seemed unremovable, and pushing the frontier of accomplishment further—what joy is there like unto it?

Keep your face to the sunshine and you cannot see the shadow.

[Once] a man was dismissed from a government position because he allowed his wife to henpeck him. I am speculating as to whether there is not some truth in the contention that if he cannot stand up before his wife he lacks the ironclad spirit required for heavy responsibilities in public life.

Human actions are shaped by a thousand forces stronger than the written wisdom of the wisest guide that ever lived.

The best educated human being is the one who understands most about the life in which he is placed.

We still have it in our power to rise above our fears, imagined and real, and to shoulder the great burdens which destiny has placed upon us.

We can do anything we want to do if we stick to it long enough.

[On beautiful women:] Their ambition is physical perfection, and in its pursuit they are starving their minds and stunting their souls. The only truly beautiful women have well-stored minds, poise, strength for serious discussion and a gift of blending laughter with fragrance of the heart.

Impatient with frustration, we ask ourselves why terrible obstacles should be placed in our path! We cannot but wonder at times why we cannot have smooth sailing instead of being compelled always to fight against adverse winds and rough seas. No doubt the reason is that character cannot be developed in ease and quiet. Only through experiences of trial and suffering can the soul be strengthened, vision cleared, ambition inspired and success achieved. Most of the men and women honored in history for their service to mankind were acquainted with "the uses of adversity." They triumphed because they refused to be turned aside by difficulties or opposition. These obstructions called forth their latent energies and the determination that carried them far beyond any goal to which they would otherwise have aspired.

History teaches us that fleets and armies are as provocative as weapons openly carried by private citizens, and that the innumerable treaties signed after wars have settled nothing.

Face your deficiencies and acknowledge them; but do not let them master you. Let them teach you patience, sweetness, insight. True education combines intellect, beauty, goodness and the greatest of these is goodness.

Knowledge is power. Rather, knowledge is happiness, because to have knowledge—broad, deep knowledge—is to know true ends from false, and lofty things from low. To know the thoughts and deeds that have marked man's progress is to feel the great heart throbs of humanity through the centuries; and if one does not feel in these pulsations a heavenward striving, one must indeed be deaf to the harmonies of life.

[On the statement that a woman's place is in the home:] Having observed the discontent, the instability and aimlessness of many "free" women in my country, I wonder if [that] may not be right to a large extent.

On Spring

There is so much to be thankful for! The feeling of springtime promise in the air after the cold grayness of the winter season; the drops of rain that take on new meaning. They are not the dull accompaniment to a somber, gray sky and a relentless chill, but bear the promise of new life and renewed energy to the rootlets and buds.

We fear to take a new step and face the consequences. If we had the secret that opens the buds, we could not help being new men and women any more than the flowers can help being new and lovely.

It is unpardonable to know the Vision Beautiful and to live falsely and selfishly. Renewal implies courage to take the initiative, to speak out the truth when others are silent, to foster love instead of hate, to put away small interests and prejudices for large sympathies, to serve others no matter what they think or do.

Columbus saw a new continent beyond uncharted seas. If he had only *believed* in its existence, and had spread no sail for the unknown shores, he would not have discovered this land we call America.

The listening ear of faith hears again the Voice of Jesus proclaiming the victory of Life over Death. "Go and tell the Brethren I am risen," He said to Mary, and with every return of Easter the human soul is renewed by His Message.

You hear the inward call to newness of life in the resurrection time—let us heed it and rise to higher planes of being.

Let us look steadfastly across the waste of grime and fraud, blood and tears, to a new continent of manhood and womanhood. Let us dare to breast the waves of hardship which beetle down upon our soul's prow. Let us trust the Christ who stilled the tempest and steered the ship safely to port.

Precious as are all the seasons of the year, none so rejoices the heart as Spring. There is about Spring a gladness that thrills the soul and lifts it up into regions of spiritual sunshine.

If we open our minds fully to that message our lives, like the earth, undergo a transformation of beauty. A wish to renew our feelings and thoughts inundates us like the sap in the trees; we long to take hold of life's problems with new emotions and fresh faculties. But the trouble is, we seldom go further than wishing.

On Easter

*The natural world is suddenly transformed
into an orchestra of silver trumpets, singing
birds, laughing streams and a fairyland of bursting
buds. Snowdrops, crocuses, violets, primroses,
buttercups and daisies tint the earth with purple,
yellow and blue. Each tree and bush puts out
tiny leaves of tender green loveliness. It is the
festival of Eastertide, and Easter bells of joy
ring softly in every heart.*

Teach it again to us, O living God! Teach us to renew ourselves, O Jesus, Who wept bitter tears in Gethsemane.

Help us to forget the long way of pain and strife we have come, each of us dragging a cross to some Calvary in our hearts. Help us to forget the hours of utter darkness when we have lost the way. Help us to forget our hates, fears and the bitter thoughts that divide us.

Help us to remember the upclimbing will that is a staff unto our feet. Nourish in us every tiny impulse to help each other. Give us more love, more compassion, more sincerity one to another.

Help us to appreciate the present moment and to search out its advantages that we may be glad for the todays of life, leaving the tomorrows in Thy Hand.

Steady us to do our full stint of work. Help us to rise each day with new sympathies, new thoughts of unity and joy.

Great need have we, this year of all years, to seek the garden where Thou, O Risen Lord, shalt lay on each heart Thy healing Hand.

Give to those who feel downtrodden and neglected the spirit to look up to the sun, to feel its warmth and to appreciate its bright rays. Let them see rainbows in the murky pools, and help them to feel that they are not alone, that Thou from Thy

Heavenly Home are watching over them.

Let us be thankful for the resurrection season which revives in us the faith that this circumscribed world in which we live, with its partial visions and unfulfilled dreams, its wearisome struggles and frustrations, is not all there is to life. There is so much to live for! There is the courageous, useful and unselfish life.

There is much to strive for—to make our cities clean and pleasant, to keep our children healthy, and teach them the honor of work that is worthy of the finest manhood and womanhood, to eradicate from all the fountains of our national life everything that is corrupt. When these commandments of life are kept, there will be resurrection in our souls and in our nation, and our days of tribulation will not have been in vain.

Well may the earth rejoice, lift her head and turn her face to the sun! The sun! The sun that mounts the heavens and makes all things new again!

On Christmas

*Light the world's Christmas tree with stars.
Heap offerings upon the mighty branches. Bring
the Yule log to the world-fireplace. Deck the world-
house with holly and mistletoe and proclaim
everywhere the Christmas of the human race.*

The legend tells that when Jesus was born the sun danced in the sky, and the aged trees straightened themselves and put on leaves and sent forth the fragrance of blossoms once more. These are the symbols of what takes place in our hearts when the Christ child is born anew each year. Blessed by the Christmas sunshine, our natures, perhaps long leafless, bring new love, new kindness, new mercy, new compassion. As the birth of Jesus was the beginning of the Christian life, so the unselfish joy at Christmas shall start the spirit that is to rule the new year.

Christmas is the harvest time of love. Souls are drawn to other souls. All that we have read and thought and hoped comes to fruition at this happy time. Our spirits are astir. We feel within us a strong desire to serve. A strange, subtle force, a new kindness, animates man and child. A new spirit is growing in us. No longer are we content to relieve pain, to sweeten sorrow, to give the crust of charity. We dare to give friendship, service, the equal loaf of bread, and love.

For ages the Christmas bells have rung their message of peace upon earth and goodwill to all men. For ages they have summoned a sleeping world to a new life, a new ideal, a new joy.

As the birth of Jesus was the beginning of the
Christian life, so the unselfish joy at Christmas
shall start the spirit that is to rule the new year.

Hear! Today the bells and I call you to the Christmas of mankind. For it has begun, and we shall not
falter nor turn back until every man and woman
and child has a chance to live happily and to develop his mind and do the best of which he is cap-
able. Generation after generation has learned from
its mothers' lips the story of the birth of Christ, and
slowly the words have borne flower—and the fruit
is the Great Change . . . the new faith.

Hear, hear the Christmas bells! How they
answer one another from end to end of the country,
peal upon peal, chime upon chime! From every
spire and tower they utter the good tidings of great
joy, the tidings of the Great Change, the cry that
no human heart can resist: "Brotherhood! Brotherhood! Brotherhood!"

I hear someone ask: "What pleasure can Christmas hold for children who cannot see their gifts or
the sparkling tree or the ruddy smile of Santa
Claus?" The question would be answered if you
could see the Christmas of the blind children. The
only really blind person at Christmastime is he who
has not Christmas in his heart.

Hear, O, hear the Christmas bells as they greet the sun, the frost, the sailing cloud, the roving wind! Are they not the bells of your brightest memories; the bells of your highest hope?

In Christmas we celebrate the birth of Him who bestowed faith upon us as a responsibility and gave us the dreams of a freer, nobler humanity which lies in us like summer in the heart of winter. It costs us an effort to tune our minds to "peace on earth and goodwill to men," but we cannot evade the beautiful summons. For it envisions our future, and our quenchless longing to live in it puts us there for a little while.

Acknowledgments

Designed by J. William Burdett.
Set in Monotype Walbaum, a light, open typeface
designed by Justus Erich Walbaum (1768-1839),
a type founder at Goslar and at Weimar.
Printed on Hallmark Eggshell Book paper.